Poetry Builders

Luke and Leo Build a
LIMERICK

by Marybeth Mataya
illustrated by Ilene Richard

Content Consultant
Kris Bigalk
Director of Creative Writing
Normandale Community College

NORWOOD HOUSE PRESS
CHICAGO, ILLINOIS

Norwood House Press
P.O. Box 316598
Chicago, Illinois 60631
For information regarding Norwood House Press, please visit
our website at:
www.norwoodhousepress.com or call 866-565-2900.

Editor: Melissa York
Designer: Emily Love
Project Management: Red Line Editorial

Library of Congress Cataloging-in-Publication Data
Mataya, Marybeth.
  Luke and Leo build a limerick / by Marybeth Mataya ; illus-
trated by Ilene Richard.
       p. cm. -- (Poetry builders)
  Includes bibliographical references.
  Summary: "Luke and Leo, with some help from Lizzie and
her sister, have fun writing Limericks. Includes creative writing
exercises to assist the reader in writing limericks"--Provided
by publisher.
  ISBN-13: 978-1-59953-436-7 (lib. ed. : alk. paper)
  ISBN-10: 1-59953-436-3 (lib. ed. : alk. paper)
  1. Limericks, Juvenile. 2. Children's poetry, American. 3.
Children's poetry--Authorship. I. Richard, Ilene, ill. II. Title.
  PN6231.L5M38 2011
  811'.5'4--dc22
                         2010043867

Words in **black bold** are defined in the glossary.

"Why Poems Aren't So Bad"

My friend Luke and I used to think we hated poems. Then Mrs. Garcia told us songs we like on our iPods are poems. That's cool. We like those!

Our favorite poems are the funny ones. Especially the limericks! They have five lines. Three sort of gallop. The middle two lines are short and snappy. And Mrs. G. calls the last line a twist—something you wouldn't expect. Like this one:

There was an old man of Blackheath
Who sat on his set of false teeth
Said he, with a start,
"Oh Lord, bless my heart!
I've bitten myself underneath!"

Some of it sounds kind of weird, but I still like it. Limericks are my new favorite way to tell jokes!

By Leo the Limericker, age 11

"Quick, Luke," croaked Leo from behind the garbage can. "Ring the doorbell and run!"

Luke jammed the paper under a rock, slapped the doorbell, and off they zipped, grinning.

Just then, a teenager with ear buds in her ears danced out. The boys spied her from behind the neighbor's bushes. "Hey, Lizzie," she hollered, waving the paper. "You've got a love note. Look at this—"

There once was a girl named Lizzie
Whose giggle was light and fizzy
Just tickle her nose
Or her pink-painted toes
She'll laugh and she'll laugh 'till she's dizzy!

Liz's older sister, Jill, cracked up. "That's a great limerick! They've got your laugh right," she called out, erupting in her own laugh. "Hey, they added:

'Happy Poetry Month

April Fools!

Guess who?!'

So who is it, Lizzie? Bet it's a boy!"

Lizzie dashed out and snatched the note. "Give it to me!"

Reading the poem, she started to giggle too, until her eyes watered and her nose snorted. Lizzie waved the paper in the air. "I know it's you guys! Leo and Luke, get over here. Tell me how you wrote this! I want to do one, too!"

"You'll have to catch us!" they yelled, sprinting away. Lizzie shot after them, until they were all panting at the park down the block. She managed to tag Luke's shirt. "Now tell!"

"There once was a girl named Lizzie," sang out Leo, as he climbed a tree.

"Who ran fast until she grew dizzy

She couldn't catch me

Or hang from a tree . . ."

"Can too!" sputtered Lizzie, out of breath.

Jill followed them to the park. She plopped down in the grass under a tree and pulled out a magazine.

Leo wiggled in the air, upside down. "Man . . . I'm stuck with the ending. Lizzy, dizzy, busy?"

"Missy?" suggested Luke, lying on the grass.

"No," argued Leo. "That doesn't really **rhyme** with Lizzie and dizzy."

Lizzie pranced in front of them as if she were in a ball gown. "How about *because she was just too ritzy!* That's what I am— so cool I could be invited to dinner at the White House."

"Yeah, sure," smirked Leo. "How about
Because she was all in a tizzy!" He dropped
out of the tree.

"Hmmph," said Lizzie, heading toward
the swings. "So what are the rules for a
limerick? I can hear that the lines rhyme."

Luke and Leo followed. Leo explained, "There are always five lines. The first two lines rhyme. The middle two lines rhyme with each other. End it all with a funny sentence that rhymes with the first one. Like this one I memorized from the Internet:

There was an old man from Peru

Who dreamt he was eating his shoe.

He awoke in a fright

In the middle of the night

And found it was perfectly true."

"I know an old limerick," added Jill, looking up from her magazine.

"There was an Old Man on the Border,

Who lived in the utmost disorder;

He danced with the Cat,

And made Tea in his Hat,

Which vexed all the folks on the Border."

"That's fun," said Lizzie, pumping her swing, "kind of old-sounding and bouncy."

"Yeah," agreed Leo. "Someone probably made up the very first limerick while he was riding a horse."

"Maybe it was a *she*," Lizzie retorted.

"The poem's by Edward Lear, a famous limerick writer," said Jill.

"That ending is kind of lame," said Luke. "What about, *It made him an awesome snowboarder?*"

"That's much better," agreed Lizzie.

"Limericks first started in Limerick, Ireland,"
Jill pointed out. "That's where they got their
name."

Jill spotted some chalk on the sidewalk where other kids had made some pictures. "I have one starting in my head. Want to see it?"

"Okay, sure," Leo said.

Jill grabbed the chalk and started scratching it against the pavement. She tried erasing with her hand, but that made a big smudge. So, she just kept moving and starting over, smudging as she went. When she was done, she had moved seven times.

"Okay, ready?" Jill said at last. She stepped aside to reveal her poem.

There once was a girl from Hong Kong
Who wanted to write a new song.
She pondered and thought
But all that she got—
A song only one sentence long!

"I like reading them out loud," Luke said. "They have a funky beat."

"Kind of like this?" Jill tapped her knees as she said, "duh DAH duh duh DAH duh duh DAW. . . . There ONCE was a GIRL from Hong KONG."

"Yeah!" Luke said.

"That's the **rhythm** for the long lines—lines one, two, and five."

"Let me guess the short lines," Luke said. He whispered to himself for a minute. Then he slowly said, "She PON-dered and THOUGHT . . . duh DAH duh duh DAH."

"You got it!" Jill said.

21

"Well, I just go by if it sounds right," Lizzie said. She cleared her throat dramatically. "Ladies and gentleman, your attention please!" With one arm waving in the air, she recited:

"There once was an odd boy named Luke,

Who acted like he was a duke."

She paused, thinking.

"Mouth open to chew

He should live in a zoo

'Cuz he makes all of his friends want to puke!"

Leo clapped and whistled. Luke just smirked. "The last line doesn't have a great rhythm, though. Try Leo."

"Okay, let's see," mused Lizzie. "How about:

I knew a kid, Leo the Slow,

But he liked to wear a Speedo . . ."

"No way!" cried Leo.

"Okay, okay," said Lizzie, standing up with her head tilted as if she were performing on a stage. "This is my old fashioned one instead:

There once was a lass named Marie,

Who went on a ship in the sea

It gave her a fright

It sank in the night

She's got to swim home now, you see!"

"Excellent!" Luke cheered, as Lizzie bowed.

Leo scowled playfully. "Guess you've got it figured out. It's my turn now. This is one I wrote for school:

There once was a nice man named Chuck

Who was pretty much out of luck.

In his bathroom stall—

Was no paper at all!

And so that poor guy is still stuck!"

"Ewww," exclaimed Lizzie. Luke clapped as Leo bowed.

"Hey, we forgot to tell her something," Leo said, nudging Luke. "Mrs. G. said it can be fun to use the same letters to begin words. She called it a-litter of cats or something."

"**Alliteration**," corrected Jill, laughing.

"Right," agreed Leo. "I memorized the one I liked best with alliteration—oh, but first I have to tell you, or you won't get it, that a flue is like a chimney. So here it is:

A fly and a flea in a flue

Were imprisoned, so what could they do?

Said the fly, 'Let us flee!'

'Let us fly!' said the flea.

So they flew through a flaw in the flue."

"And that will do!" giggled Lizzie.

You Can Write a Limerick, too!

Limericks have five lines. Lines one, two, and five are long. Three and four are shorter. Lines one and two rhyme with each other. Lines three and four rhyme with each other. Then, line five rhymes with lines one and two. Limericks have a rhythm that makes you want to tap your feet.

Writing limericks is fun! First, write down the names of some people or places you like. Write down some words that rhyme with them.

Brazil, Jill, ill, fill, kill, bill, thrill, spill, still

Many limericks follow the same pattern for their first line: "There once was a ___ named ___" or "There once was a ___ from ___." You can use this pattern if you like.

After you finish your first line, read it out loud. Does it have a good beat? Then find a rhyming word to write your second line.

There once was a cat from Brazil
Who went to Peru for a thrill.

Next, play around with some different words that rhyme to make two shorter matching lines.

> He drifted to sea
> Where he felt so free

Now think of an unexpected and funny ending. And remember, the last word has to rhyme with the end of your two first lines. Say:

> But sad there were no mice to kill!

Now read it aloud a few times to see if it works for you.

> There once was a cat from Brazil
> Who went to Peru for a thrill.
> He drifted to sea
> Where he felt so free,
> But sad there were no mice to kill!

That works . . . but can you do better?

Glossary

alliteration: the repeating of words that begin with the same sound.

rhyme: a word that shares the end sounds of another word but has a different beginning—like dust, must, rust, and fussed.

rhythm: the pattern of sounds in a poem, like a drumbeat.

For More Information

Books

Brooks, Lou. *Twimericks: The Book of Tongue-Twisting Limericks*. New York: Workman Publishing, 2009.

Bull, Webster. *A Kittery Kayaker*. Beverly, MA: Commonwealth, 2007.

Prelutsky, Jack. *Pizza, Pigs, and Poetry: How to Write a Poem*. New York: Greenwillow Books, 2008.

Websites

The Edward Lear Homepage
www.nonsenselit.org/Lear/
This website features the limericks of Edward Lear, a famous poet from the nineteenth century.

Rhyme Zone
www.rhymezone.com
This website is a rhyming dictionary. Enter any word and it will produce many words that rhyme with it.

About the Author

Marybeth Mataya is a writer and a teacher of writing and children's literature at the University of Wisconsin–River Falls.

About the Illustrator

Ilene Richard has a long list of children's books to her credit and has worked with many well-known educational and trade publishers in the United States.